The Ten Commandments

Text
Sr. Karen Cavanagh, C.S.J.

Illustrations
Rita Goodwill

Cover Illustration
Michael Letwenko

THE REGINA PRESS
New York

FREEDOM
FOR GOD'S PEOPLE

The people of Israel had been in slavery for many years. God called a man named Moses to lead them to freedom.

One day God spoke to Moses from a bush that was on fire but did not burn up. God called, "Moses! Moses!" Moses answered, "Here I am."

"Remove your sandals," said God, "you are standing on holy ground." Then God said, "I want you to lead my people to freedom in a new land—a land of promise. Go to the people and say, 'I AM' sent me.

This is my name for all time—for every generation."

I AM

OUR FAITHFUL GOD

During the long journey to their freedom, the people sometimes were afraid that God—I AM—would not help them.

The God—I AM—wanted the people to know that they were not alone. Both day and night they knew God was close by them.

The many signs seemed to be saying to the people of Israel:

I AM with you.
   I AM always near.
I AM your protector.
   I AM your shelter.
I AM your nourishment.
   I AM your savior.
I AM your friend.
   I AM your God.

God says this to you and me, too!

THE TEN COMMANDMENTS

After the long journey, God told Moses to tell the people, "I AM the one who carried you here—you are my Chosen Ones, dearer than all others."

The people said, "We also love our God."

Having made a lasting promise of love, God called Moses to climb Mount Sinai. Here upon the mountain God gave Moses the Ten Commandments.

God said, "I AM your God who brought you to freedom. These are my commandments, which you are to obey."

Moses received the commandments, which were written on two stone tablets.

Moses became the teacher of the "Law of Love," which God gives all of us.

THE FIRST COMMANDMENT

Love God Above All Else— Do Not Have False Gods.

God is the Maker of our world who created each one of us. God wants us to live knowing we are loved and that God is always near.

The First Commandment tells us to remember always God's care for us. God says, "My love will always be enough for you."

Sometimes we forget God's promise and make other persons or things more important than our God.

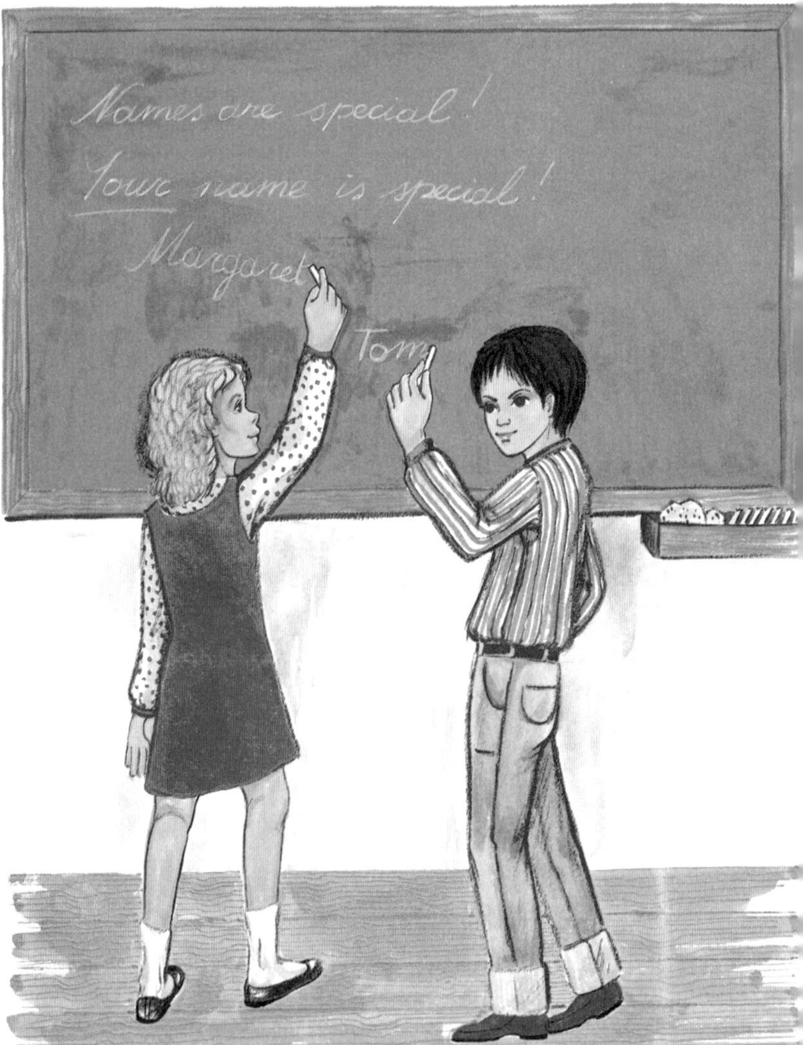
Names are special!
Your name is special!
Margaret
Tom

THE SECOND COMMANDMENT

Love and Respect God's Name— Do Not Take God's Name in Vain

Names are special! Your name is very special because it means you. It is one of the first things you learn to spell and write.

God says, "I call you by name!"

No one should dishonor anyone's name—especially God's name.

We should:
  Speak it with respect.
  Pray it with reverence.
  Call upon it with love.

THE THIRD COMMANDMENT

Remember the Lord's Day— Keep It Holy.

Because you are so important, God wants you to have a day of rest, a day to remember who you are, where you come from, and how much you are loved. Our sabbath day, our Lord's Day is Sunday.

God wants to spend part of this day with us. That is why we go to church with our family and friends. On Sunday we listen to God's Word; we share the bread of Eucharist; we pray for each other.

THE FOURTH COMMANDMENT

Honor Your Father and Your Mother.

God shares the special work of creation with your Father and your Mother. God asks them to show what love is like by the way they care for you and by their love for each other.

They are your first and best teachers. They teach you who God is and how God loves you.

Sometimes others take the place of parents in our lives. They, too, deserve honor and respect.

THE FIFTH COMMANDMENT

Honor All Life— Do Not Kill.

Life is a wonderful and beautiful mystery. It is a gift to be enjoyed; it is precious and deserves care and respect.

We obey this Fifth Commandment when we honor others—when we do not kill the special moments of joy in another person's life by being disrespectful, by fighting, or by doing things that make us forget that someone else's life is precious.

THE SIXTH COMMANDMENT

Do Not Commit Adultery.

This commandment is mostly for married people. When two people marry, they promise to share their bodies and spirits with each other. They must keep that promise to each other.

This Commandment reminds others who are not married to always honor and care for their bodies and to be sincere with their friends.

When we promise to be a true friend, we should not break our promise, and we should not lead another to break a promise.

THE SEVENTH COMMANDMENT

Respect Each Other's Property— Do Not Steal or Cheat.

We all have things that are our very own. Some of them are special because of whom or where they came from. Others are special because we've worked hard for them or waited a long time for them. We would never want another to take them from us.

To take something from another is harmful, selfish, and wrong. Everyone has a right to what belongs to them.

When we cheat at school or play, we also take what is not ours.

THE EIGHTH COMMANDMENT

Be Truthful at All Times— Do Not Lie.

God wants us always to be happy. The truth brings happiness. Lies hurt and bring sadness.

Lying might sometimes seem to get us out of trouble, but often someone else gets hurt. When we lie, our self respect always gets hurt. Ask someone to tell you about the boy who cried, "Wolf."

When we talk about others' secrets or business (even when what we say is true), we hurt them and hurt our own selves.

THE NINTH COMMANDMENT

Honor Your Neighbor's Wife— Do Not Be Jealous.

On special days, we realize how happy gifts make us. They are always a reminder of another's love for us.

This Commandment reminds us that married people give each other the gift of themselves as husband and wife. The love and happiness this gift brings is very special.

God does not want any man or woman to desire or to take away this gift from any other man or woman.

THE TENTH COMMANDMENT

Honor Your Neighbor's Goods— Do Not be Jealous or Greedy.

Often someone else has something good, and we might wish it was our own. We all would like to have special things, to be talented at sports or school, to have nice clothes, to be popular.

To want good or nice things for ourselves is alright. It becomes wrong when we become unhappy or mean because someone else has what we would like.

We should be happy for them and thankful for the goods and gifts that we do have.

GOD'S LAW
OF LOVE

God's Law of Love—God's Ten Commandments—have been given to the many generations of God's people. They have been taught to God's people throughout the thousands of years since Moses received them on Mount Sinai. They have probably been written in every language that is spoken.

When Jesus was on earth, He preached the message of God's lasting promise. He was the teacher of the "New Law of Love" that God gives. He said "You shall love God with all your being and your neighbor as yourself."

Jesus' "New Law of Love" was one more way of helping us take responsibility for our freedom. We are freed to be one people united in love.

The Ten Commandments are ways that we can show our love for God and for our neighbor.

The stone tablets that had the Ten Commandments written on them have been lost. We can read them in the Bible and in the books in our school or church, but the best place to read them is in our hearts. They will become written in our hearts as we obey them and show God our love.